The Special Needs Parenting Survival Guide

Erik Young, M.Ed., LPC

Erik Young, M.Ed., LPC

ISBN: 0615880037
ISBN-13: 978-0615880037

DEDICATION

This book is dedicated to all the special parents and special kids that
inspired its content. May you find hope and peace within these pages.

Erik Young, M.Ed., LPC

CONTENTS

Erik Young, M.Ed., LPC

ACKNOWLEDGMENTS

First and foremost I have to thank my wife, Lorrie. Your support, love and understanding truly made this possible. I still can't believe you chose me. I also want to thank all my children without whom I couldn't have learned what I needed to know to put this book together.

I also wish to thank Rand and Michele, your mentorship, friendship and help has been invaluable. Someday I hope to pay your good deeds forward.

Erik Young, M.Ed., LPC

INTRODUCTION

This is book is for parents, siblings, grandparents, guardians… anyone… who loves someone with "special needs", specifically, autism, intellectual disability, and emotional/behavioral issues. I was once told that becoming a parent of a child with special needs is like winning a lottery to which you didn't buy a ticket.

> ➤ It can be scary, surprising, exhilarating and frustrating.
> ➤ All the advice handed down from well-meaning family and friends is often unhelpful at best.
> ➤ Chances are, no one in your social circle can truly empathize with your situation and the needs of your child.
> ➤ Most of all, it can be lonely.

Sounds pretty bleak, right? Here's the thing… YOU ARE NOT ALONE. Raising a child with special needs is hard. There are few things more challenging. However, it IS possible and you are up to the task (whether you know it or not). In this book:

> ➤ You will hear from me and other parents who have been where you are right now.
> ➤ You will learn how to create and strengthen an effective social support system that will allow you to:
>> A. <u>Care for your child</u> and
>> B. <u>Find some joy and balance in your life</u>.

What this book is…

This book is:

> ➤ A collection of guidelines and anecdotes from me about the road you are travelling now.

It is geared primarily toward:

> ➤ Parents dealing with issues surrounding autism, intellectual disability and emotional/behavior disorders

It is meant to:

> ➤ Help you formulate your <u>own</u> solutions for your unique situation.
> ➤ Grant guidance and hopefully show you that major parts of your unique situation are shared by others as well as give you practical solutions to common situations.

What this book is not...

> ➤ This book is not a plan of treatment for any specific condition
> ➤ This book is NOT a collection of RULES!!
> > o If something in this book doesn't speak to you or does not fit your situation, no worries...

> **Identify the principles behind the guidelines and create guidelines for yourself that work best for you.**

How this book is set up...

> ➤ This book has two parts.
> > o **Part one** lays out my guidelines for creating your social safety net. It's the "meat and potatoes" of this book.
> > o **Part two** is a bonus collection of articles I've written geared toward special needs parenting and stress management. These articles may provide you with extra tools for your Special Needs Parenting Toolkit.

> ➤ To get the most out of this book:
> > o Read Part 1 in its entirety and then
> > o Read whatever you find interesting or most useful in the rest of the book.

About me...

My name is Erik Young. This book is the culmination of my current knowledge and experience about parenting children with special needs. I started working with individuals with Traumatic Brain injury back in 1993. It wasn't my intention to get into the mental health field. At the time I was planning on being a professional musician, but I needed a job to support my music habit. I didn't imagine I would be any good at helping people, but it turned out that I had a knack for working with people who needed special consideration (lack of social skills, impulsive, etc.). I pursued psychology alongside my music studies and continued working in jobs that had me working with adults and children with various special needs all the way through music school. I eventually relegated music to a serious hobby and continued my studies in counseling and human services to further my career.

By 2001, I finished my Master's degree and started working with children and adults with autism and intellectual disability at a residential treatment center. A few years later, I crossed over from doing treatment to parenting (which is perhaps the most powerful of treatments). That was when my wife and I started providing specialized foster care for children with IDD and Autism in our household.

I quickly found out that a lot of what I "knew" was useful... but needed tweaking to work in our house. I also learned that there was a TON of stuff I hadn't learned; stuff that wasn't covered in classes, training, and therapy work outside the home . I had many successes and also made some mistakes. I tried to learn from all of it. My deepest wish is that some of this experience will speak to you, and that you will find something useful that will improve your situation and bring some relief and happiness to you and your family.

Free Bonus Content...

I have a series of worksheets and other bonus content to go with this book. If you would like this content, simply email me at erikyounglpc@verizon.net and put Parenting Bonus Content in the subject.

Part One: The Social Safety Net Plan

THE BASIC SURVIVAL STEPS (OVERVIEW)

A colleague once told me that becoming the parent of a special needs child is like winning the lottery in which you didn't buy a ticket. We all come to this journey in different ways… birth of a child, fostering or adoption of a child, perhaps even parenting a neurotypical child who then develops a condition due to accident or illness. No matter the how we came to be here, it's a safe bet this is not what we planned for. Furthermore, if you are reading this book, you probably have some questions about what to do now that you are here.

While it is true, that every situation is different, even people with similar diagnoses vary greatly in how they express their condition and therefore have different needs.. Different families have different resources based on familial make up (single parent versus extended family for example), financial situation, geographic location (what services are available in your area?) and the like. Bottom line, yours is a unique situation unlike any other person's situation… but there seem to be some universal issues that we share. Thus, there are some basic guidelines that can help just about any family in any situation.

NOTE: Throughout this book I will be referring to anecdotes from my experiences of other families. In all cases I have changed the names of those mentioned to protect their identities and maintain confidentiality.

So, without further ado, here are my basic survival guidelines:

> **Don't Panic!**

> **Get educated**

> **Take inventory (what are your resources)**

> **Identify and educate your support team (expand your resources)**

> **Hook up with available community resources (expand your resources)**

> **Strive for balance**

> **Again… Don't Panic!**

This list of guidelines based on my 20 years of training and experience. However, I want to share with you the story of the inspiration for much of this system. This is the story of a family that I worked for early in my career. To this day, they stand out as the model of a family who really did things right.

> *This is the story of a family that I worked for early in my career. To this day, they stand out as the model of a family who really did things right.*

Back in 1995, I was midway through my undergraduate program. My family and I had just moved to a new town so I could go to a new college to complete my bachelor's program. I quickly landed a part-time job working as an aide in the home of this family helping them provide care for their adult son, Perry. This job was life changing. Through this family I eventually made the connections that got me into graduate school, which then led to my work at Devereux. More importantly, I got to see outcomes very different from what I was seeing at my other jobs.

At my university job, I worked with a lot of individuals who had spent their lives in state mental hospitals. They received little nurture and were exposed to intense abuse and neglect. While all of these people were great people, they were challenging to work with. They had developed intense behaviors to deal with bizarre and unusual situations.

On the other hand, Perry' mother did not listen to the advice of her doctors to put her young son into the same type of hospitals. Despite a lack of support and services, she and her husband chose to keep Perry home and raise him at home. He was raised in a loving and nurturing environment. His parents educated the rest of their extended family and created a strong family support system for Perry. Mom then went out and advocated to get the services in place that she figured her son would need. Her work was instrumental in bringing the ARC to their county. She got him special schooling, but fought for as much inclusion as she could get (she is a teacher by profession).

When I came into their lives, I was one of four other staff who came to their house to take Perry out into the community and do activities with him. We assisted with his daily living skills. Mom and Dad supervised us closely, but they also welcomed us as part of the extended family that supported Perry. Despite the challenges of raising and caring for Perry, they had a nice house, careers, a meaningful family and social life… and they were always there for Perry. In short, they achieved balance. Perry thrived. He was safe and well cared for. He did not develop many of the bizarre behaviors that my clients from the state hospital system displayed.

After I left their service and moved on with my career, I always looked back at my time with Perry as an example of a family that did a LOT of things right. They really are the standard I hold myself to as far as raising special needs kids goes. Without their inspiration, I wouldn't be writing this book… heck, I wouldn't be the kind of professional I am today. For this,

Perry and his family have my deepest thanks.

1. DON'T PANIC!

Winning the Lottery

As was said earlier, becoming the parent of a special needs child is a little like winning a lottery to which you didn't buy a ticket. It's something that changes your life and there is no way you can be totally prepared for what is going to happen. Your new life path will be full of unexpected challenges, but also full of unimaginable joy (if you open your heart to it). Basically, you face a great deal of change (and change = stress with a capital **S**) which you did not sign up for.

When I am faced with a great deal of stress (and thus change)… the first thing I need to do is follow the great advice of the author Douglas Adams in his fantastic book "Hitchhiker's Guide to the Galaxy." (A must read so far as I am concerned) – DON'T PANIC.

Panic activates the sympathetic nervous system (associated with the so-called fight-or-flight response). When this happens, your body is preparing for a perceived life-or-death struggle. Unfortunately, though you are not in a dire life-or-death struggle, your stressors are going to be long-lasting. Therefore, you don't need to fight them so much as you need to eliminate, minimize or learn to live with them. The fight-or-flight reaction simply sucks energy in preparing the body to deal with life or death situations. Right now, the last thing you want to do is use up all of your energy. You need to stay calm, think, plan...get in touch with the ever-so-relaxed parasympathetic nervoussysteme… there will be plenty of opportunities to make use of the sympathetic nervous system later (trust me!)

> **Quick Tip!**
> Just remember this little mantra *"Breathe!...You got this."* It's what I remind myself when I start to feel panic. This reminds me to put the panic aside and put energy towards finding solutions.

Good enough parenting - there is no way to do this perfectly.

It's unfair. Many parents strive to be perfect. They go to great lengths not to screw things up. Unfortunately, it seems that the harder you strive for perfection, the more you mess things up.

Actually, I take that back. It's not that you screw up more often, it's just that when you do (and you will) the harder you will fall. It's about the dissonance... the disconnect between your desire and your reality.

I strive for and counsel my clients to be "good enough" parents.

> *Raising a child is hard...raising a child with special needs is harder. Don't add to your challenges with an unrealistic world view. Do your best. Be good enough. If you do this, you and your child will thrive.*

> ➤ Good enough parents love their children.
> ➤ Good enough parents try to make the right decisions for themselves and their kids.
> ➤ Good enough parents do the best they can with what they've got.
> ➤ Good enough parents make mistakes. However, they learn from their mistakes.
> ➤ They try not to repeat their mistakes and they constantly strive to be better today than they were yesterday. If you make this your parenting goal (or even just a general life goal), you set yourself up to be happier and more successful in the long run.

A perfect parent is doomed to fail (for just one little mistake or oversight ruins perfection). Not only that, once that failure happens… they can no longer be a perfect parent. On the other hand, a Good Enough parent might fail. Given how hard it is to raise kids, it's a good bet (I've yet to meet a perfect parent), BUT a good enough parent is allowed, by definition, to fail. This means that after the failure, they can fix things up… maybe learn a thing or two… and still be a good enough parent. They can even learn from the failure and become a BETTER parent. *This* is something denied to the mindset of the perfect parent.

Raising a child is hard…. raising a child with special needs is harder. Don't add to your challenges with an unrealistic world view. Do your best. Be good enough. If you do this, you and your child will thrive.

> *Remember, DON'T PANIC. You are NOT alone. While your situation is unique… you are not the only parent of a child with his/her particular condition.*

It's Do-able

It may seem impossible right now. There's so much you don't know. Maybe you're getting a whole lot of information thrown at you all at once… much of it contradictory. Maybe you can't conceive of how your life is going to change and how you are going to make everything work.

Remember, DON'T PANIC. You are NOT alone. While your situation is unique… you are not the only parent of a child with his/her particular condition. If you were truly alone… I would not have written this book. There are other parents out there facing similar struggles and probably feeling similar worries and doubts. There are probably more than a few very close to where you live. Also, with the wonders of the internet and social networking, you don't even need to just find them in your hometown.

You can connect with fellow parents all over the world. DO IT. You don't need to do this thing alone... in fact, if you try to do it alone; it's going to be harder for yu. Parents that are further down the path than you can serve as a source of knowledge, mentorship and inspiration. Parents newer to the path (coming up behind you) can benefit from your knowledge and experience. At the end of the day, other people have done and are doing what you want to do... if they can do it, there is no reason you cannot do it.

Erik Young, M.Ed., LPC

2. GET EDUCATED

True Story!

I remember when my wife and I took in our first foster child. This young lady was one of the most damaged human beings I have ever met. I figured my training as a therapist and my experience at Devereux had me prepared to handle her trauma history and behaviors. Within a few days, it was clear that I was in over my head. I was trained to identify the function of a behavior and then either reinforce or not reinforce the behavior depending on whether or not I wanted to see it. I was trained to use nurture and clear communication to connect with people so that my efforts at behavior modification would work better. With this girl, the more we nurtured, the more we praised, the more we reinforced….the more difficult she got. Conversely, when we were stern, when we were less nurturing, the easier she got. It was as if the rules for behavior modification …everything I knew to be true…went out the window. It made me question my professional identity and my competence.

I poured my heart out to a colleague and friend about this. He asked me what I knew about "attachment." I recall saying I'd heard about it in school and that this was comprised of two or three paragraphs in a couple of basic psychology texts. My friend then educated me about the realities of *Reactive Attachment Disorder*, its prevalence in the foster care/adoption community, and the realities of living with someone who had this. He was the parent of two adoptive kids with significant abuse histories. He was able to guide me in how better to handle this child. The moral of the tale is that I *thought* I knew what I was doing. Despite all my education and training, I was ill prepared for the reality that faced me. Getting educated is what allowed me to do a better job and make better decisions in the long run.

****

Unless you happen to be an expert on your child's particular condition (and even if you think you are), you probably will not know much about it. In fact, it's a safe bet that this thing your child has is not something you ever thought about much in your entire life. Now, it's liable to consume a lot of your waking thoughts. Rather than sitting there spinning your wheels in ignorance… you are going to want to get up to speed on what your child has. How common is it? What is the probable course of the condition? What is life like living with the condition? What are the best treatments for it? These questions and more are worth answering.

If my experience with this is any indication, a quick Google search is going to give you hundreds if not thousands of hits about this thing you previously knew nothing about. In all those hits will be lots of contradictory information. Understandably, this is not what you need right now… more confusion. Confusion can lead to fear… fear leads to extra stress…. extra stress is an energy drain you can't afford right now. Do me (and yourself) a favor…. take a deep breath. Say, "I got this", and just relax.

Here's what I want you to do:

1. Just start reading…. and keep reading. Check out Wikipedia, read websites, forums, find out about the major non-profits dedicated to treatment and education about the condition. **Don't try to make sense of everything at first… just take it all in.** Take notes and write down questions as they come to you. Where you note inconsistencies and contradictions… take note. Don't stress over them yet.

2. **Find out the names of professionals in your area who *are* experts in this condition. Focus on things they have written. Go to lectures**

and talks they are giving locally. Maybe even schedule an appointment to meet with them. Try to get answers to some of your questions. **Seek clarity.**

3. Talk to other parents. You can find them online in forums sponsored by the advocacy groups I mentioned earlier. There may be local support groups you can attend in your area. These parents can often give you some practical advice... they may also point you in the direction of other reliable sources of information.

Just keep repeating the above steps. The path of getting educated about this stuff will be an on-going process. You will want to stay up-to-date on the latest treatments and science regarding your situation as much as possible. You will be getting educated through all the other survival steps.

> *Less than scrupulous people will try to hide behind weak science to lend an air of credibility to what they are selling*

Reliable and Unreliable Information

Not all information is good information. Just because it was written down or reported on the internet doesn't make the information accurate. You will need to learn to sort the wheat from the chaff. There is no easy way to go about it, but the more you learn, the easier it will be to get a sense of what's good and what isn't. Here are some guidelines to help you:

➢ When comparing treatments and interventions, try to stick with those that have research support behind them.
   o Follow the references. Good reports will cite their sources. Try to locate those and read them as well.
   o Be wary of interventions based off of one study... or where all the sources point to one study. Less than

scrupulous people will try to hide behind weak science to lend an air of credibility to what they are selling.

> If it sounds too good to be true…. It probably is. Reports that promise a miraculous cure or larger-than-life improvements are risky. At the very least they are probably trying to sell you something. This may seem innocent enough (and desperate parents are prone to use these interventions in an attempt to feel like they are doing something). At the very least it leads to a waste of precious time and money… at the very worst, it can cause harm to your child and/or your family.

****

True Story!

A classic example is Facilitated Communication (FC). In the autism community, a study was published about a communication intervention where facilitators were trained to assist non-verbal individuals with autism communicate. The theory was that inside autistic individuals was a "normal" person waiting to communicate. The facilitator would put his hand over the autistic person's hand and help them type. The training was such that the facilitator was supposed to be helping the autistic person "talk." Based on the initial study, the subjects were suddenly making great gains in their ability to talk. Desperate families flocked to this new technique and FC certifications sprang up seemingly overnight. Failed attempts to replicate the study were dismissed by the FC creator and parents raved about their child's newfound ability to communicate. Eventually, further studies conclusively demonstrated that the Facilitators were subconsciously influencing communications. The children were not communicating but rather the facilitators. In some cases, children with the help of FC made accusations of abuse against staff and their families (people went to jail), parents paid a lot of money for FC-trained staff. Worst of all, years of critical time to teach better forms of communication were lost. There are countless similar stories of other interventions that were thrown out there but did not live up to the hype. Be wary and don't let your need to do something make you try interventions that waste your time, money, energy and may be a risk for your child. Be skeptical above all else.

****

- ➢ Just because it's on the internet doesn't make it accurate.
    - o Anybody can put up a fancy website for very little money.
    - o There are people who prey on desperate parents and are willing to offer parents empty hope in order to take their money.
    - o Wikipedia can be changed by anyone.
    - o Follow the "sources" to determine the validity of what you are reading. If there aren't sources, you have to wonder why.
- ➢ Just because it's in a magazine doesn't make it accurate.
    - o Popular magazines publish stories to sell advertising. They often go with sensationalistic stories and don't dig too deeply into the science. As always, try to find the original sources.
    - o Peer reviewed journals, on the other hand, are better sources of info. These articles have been reviewed by other scientists and are more likely to have reliable info.
    - o Focus on more recent articles over older articles. Things change remarkably quickly.

Quick Tip!
Occam's Razor – this is a principle used by scientists that basically states that the simplest, most direct explanation is probably the best explanation. Keep this in mind when evaluating information.

Erik Young, M.Ed., LPC

3. TAKE INVENTORY

The next step requires some thinking and introspection. You need to figure out not just where you are with regard to your child and his/her condition, but you need to figure out what you can bring to the situation as far as resources. This is crucial. Done correctly, this step will allow you to work from a position of strength (by utilizing what you are good at) while you shore up areas that are weaknesses. You can focus your limited energies where they will have the most impact. If you don't take inventory, then you will likely be reacting randomly from crisis to crisis. There will be little, if any, planning and your stress level will go through the roof. Knowledge is power. You need knowledge of your child's condition, but you need self-knowledge as well. If you want some worksheets to help you with this step, send an email to erikyounglpc@verizon.net and put Parent Bonus Content in the subject.

> *Knowledge is power. You need knowledge of your child's condition, but you need self-knowledge as well.*

A. Strengths and weaknesses

We all have them. No one person is perfect. No one person can do it all. Ask yourself the following questions:

➢ **What kind of parent am I?**

(Permissive? Authoritarian? Nurturing? Aloof?) – There are parenting theories out there that rate parents along two dimensions, nurture and demand. **Nurturing** is how much affection is demonstrated to a child. Some parents are very demonstrative others are much more reserved. The parent is also rated on **how much demand** they put on children. Some parents are low demand and very permissive while others are high demand and expect a lot from their kids. The research seems to support an authoritative (high nurture, high demand) style of parenting as being ideal. Where do you fall? Where does your partner fall? How can you work together to create an ideal authoritative parenting environment? Do you need to make changes in your parenting style? Do you want to?

➢ **How resilient am I?**
Resiliency refers to your ability to deal with change, manage stress, and bounce back from failure/loss/disappointments. Some people are very resilient. Nothing seems to get them down. Others are very sensitive and don't handle stress and change well. If you are not very resilient… what are the things that you struggle with? Is it time management? Do you tend to want to ignore or run away from problems? Maybe you are good with certain kinds of situations that you are comfortable with, but struggle to maintain composure in novel /unfamiliar situations.

For example, my wife is very uncomfortable with sexual/puberty issues. I am not, so I do a lot more of the direct intervention with these issues. My wife is much better at leisure time/downtime programming (i.e. keeping the kids busy) than I am…. so she handles the planning and I follow her lead in these situations.

You can learn more about resiliency and do some work to improve yours by getting hold of the following book *Building Your Bounce* by Mary Mackrain and Nefertiti Bruce published by Kaplan Early Learning www.kaplanco.com

➢ **Who can I put on my team?** Your team is comprised of all the people you can count on to help you. This includes family, friends, neighbors, hired professionals, community advocates, etc. You've probably heard the phrase "it takes a village to raise a child" and your team is your village. Identify potential team members. Figure out what they are good at… what things you can rely upon them for… it's a bad idea to rely on someone for something they cannot provide. That way lies madness and disappointment…. (mostly just disappointed). Be inclusive in your list. This is not an exclusive club we are putting together here… Here is a sample of some of the people on my team:

- My wife (the co-captain…. ok, the 5 star general to my lieutenant)
- My son
- My daughter
- My Mom and stepfather
- My Dad
- My sister
- My wife's sister
- Her other sister
- Our Devereux case manager
- Other Devereux staff (like 20 different people that comprise two different schools, medical, etc.)
- Two Guardian ad litums
- Various county workers
- Various agency workers
- A special needs dentist (Dr. Z)
- Two different pediatricians
- Various specialty physicians
- Psychiatrists
- Several colleagues whom I consult with to brainstorm behavioral issues
- A handyman
- A plumber
- An electrician
- A CPA

o   A couple of neighbors
o   Other foster parents from our agency

This is not an exhaustive list. Nor did this list come together overnight. This was built up over the years. But as you can see the range of people and the services they provide is far reaching. We don't do what we do alone… far from it. In fact, all the families I know who live with special needs members have similarly rich social support networks. If you take time to build your team, your life will be easier.

> *We don't do what we do alone… far from it. In fact, all the families I know who live with special needs members have similarly rich social support networks. If you take time to build your team, your life will be easier.*

➢ **What are my money/time/work constraints?** Take a hard look at your finances. Take a look at your job. Do you have the freedom and flexibility to meet your family's needs? Will your job allow you to take time off when you need to for meetings and appointments? Do you have money set aside for emergency repairs and extra medical issues? If not, are there changes you can make to give you more time and money?

Once you've done some of this questioning, please do not panic. Remember, panic is an energy drain and doesn't lead to solutions. Start by thinking about the strengths you listed. How can you use them to meet the situation? What about the strengths of other team members? How can use working from your strengths to shore up your weaknesses? How can different team members complement each other? The tasks ahead of you may seem monumentally gigantic; too big to even comprehend. However, you don't need to fix EVERYTHING immediately. This is not a race. You have your whole life to get this stuff right. Just pick an issue and tackle it. Once done, move on to the next issue. Prioritize things so that the most pressing issues get the most work first and just keep at it. I will talk more about the "micro-change" approach later in the book.

B. Grieve the dream child – celebrate the gift child.

I have yet to meet a parent who didn't fantasize about what their child would be like from the moment they found out/decided to become a parent. This is as true for adoptive/foster parents as it is for "natural" or biological parents. In doing this, we craft for ourselves a kind of "dream child."

This dream child represents all our hopes and dreams for the future. The dream child is beautiful, perfect, athletic, easy, smart, capable, and wonderful. The dream child will do all the things we never could as adults. They will listen to all of our advice and avoid all of our failures.

Needless to say, no real child can live up to the dream child. For "neurotypical" (so-called normal) families, the dissonance (difference) between the dream child and the real child is dealt with gradually, over time. As the child grows and the parents get to know the real child (and his/her strengths and abilities) the real child supplants the dream child in the parent's world. Unfortunately, most special needs children make their differences known quickly (if not immediately)… there is no slowly getting the dream child to meld with the real child. The dissonance is jarring.

This is perhaps even truer for special needs parent by choice (aka Foster/adoptive parents). A lot of foster parents have told me they expected to help their kids and that their kids would appreciate the love, work and sacrifice. The fact that their kids often did the exact opposite of appreciating them came as a shock. It is often the first conflict new foster/adoptive parents have to tackle.

In a sense, we, as parents, need to grieve for the death of our dream child. We need to mourn for the loss of our dreams. This is ok and perfectly normal. However, eventually (as soon as reasonably possible), we need to let go of the dream and start looking at the gift of the child you have. This child, despite the challenges his needs may represent you, will give you joy.

This child IS wonderful. Avoid getting so focused on the negatives, the obstacles, the challenges that you miss the gifts. These gifts are going to be what keep you going when the going gets rough. Don't get so wrapped up in the day to day that you deny yourself the gifts (the beautiful smile, the unreserved belly laugh, the silly giggle fits, etc.). Your life may be different and challenging… but it doesn't have to be miserable.

4. IDENTIFY AND TRAIN YOUR SUPPORT TEAM

In the previous section, we mentioned making a list of all the people who can support you and your family. This section will go into more detail about how to set up and optimize your support team. This is, perhaps, one of the most important things you can do as a parent.   Under no circumstances can you allow yourself to become isolated from the rest of the world. There is no reason to do this alone.

> *Under no circumstances can you allow yourself to become isolated from the rest of the world. There is no reason to do this alone.*

A. It takes a village – optimize yours – Create a social safety net

Recall the list of people in my family's social safety net? That is my list now. It was not the list I had when we started out as special needs parents. It was pretty much me, my wife, and a caseworker. The rest of the people we gradually added over time as we found we needed them or as they came into our lives. We were pretty passive about building the list. This was a mistake.

I have a nasty habit of trying to do everything myself. I like to bootstrap my way out of trouble. I've been successful at this enough that I often don't see when I should be asking for help. **Don't be like me… ask for help whenever you need it.** Hell, ask for help when you don't need… give yourself the gift of a break now and then. There will be plenty of opportunity to be independent and do things yourself. Trust me.

Anyway, take your list of potential helpers… look at it and see if you can spot any potential areas that aren't covered by this list. Here is a list of services that need to be covered by your safety net:

➤ **Childcare** – you will need people you can trust to look after your child when you are not there (because of work, emergencies or because you need a break and want to go out). This can be covered in part by school or day programs, but also needs to include people you can count on to do babysitting.

➤ **Medical professionals** that have an understanding of your child's condition or are willing to get educated about your child's condition.

➤ **Mental health and social work professionals** -- you will want to have access to people who can help you navigate the system as far as finding services for your child and your family, people who you can turn to when things get stressful, people who understand your child's condition and what living with that condition can be like.

➤ **Home repair and maintenance specialists** -- This one is not obvious. You need to have access to a handyman, plumber and electrician. You might also want to consider getting a good drywall and paint guy. Here's the thing… my experience with special needs kids (autism, behavior disorder, adhd, etc.) tells me that these kids are very hard on their surroundings ------much more so than their neurotypical peers. It will behoove you to get some skills at basic home maintenance to save some bucks, but sooner or later you will need professional intervention to fix something your kids broke.

To give you an example of what I mean… I replace a toilet (the entire toilet mind you) at least once every year or two. In fact, I can remember vividly standing in the toilet aisle, muttering to myself (my oldest foster child had once again broken the toilet and clogged the system so badly I had to replace everything) trying to figure out what model to buy. My eyes alighted on the one claiming it could flush a bucket of golf balls without clogging. I went with that one. Most people don't have to worry about that. Most people would consider this story amusingly odd, but for me it is an example of "normal."

If money is an issue, you might look into signing up with a home warranty service. For a monthly fee, you can get most things in your house repaired for a single deductible. This will cover all sorts of appliance repairs and the like. Generally, the copay is cheaper than the cost of the repair. The downside is that you get whatever repair person the warranty person sends… and there can be a great deal of variability in the quality of their work.

➤ Legal/tax/financial advice – You won't need these people often, but you should have a good lawyer, CPA and financial advisor in mind.

B. Educate your family – They want to help, but chances are they don't know what to do. —tell them what you need.

For most new parents, their first source of support is their family. Grandma and Grandpa can't wait to watch their grandchild and they have lots of advice (most of it pertinent and useful). Everyone wants to chip in to help. I know when my first child was born; the support of our family was an invaluable godsend.

However, when your child has special needs, family can be less than helpful. All that useful advice that seems to work for a neurotypical kid is often less useful with your child, and in many cases, the advice is flat out wrong.

"He' just being stubborn, you just have to show some tough love."

"She can't possibly do that."

"Don't worry, I read about this vitamin therapy that will straighten everything out."

"There's no such thing as [insert your child's condition here]."

These are examples of advice that some of my families have received from their families. The thing is, these people really want to help. The advice they give comes from a good place, but is based on their experiences (which don't encompass the needs and challenge presented by the typical special needs child). Remember how scared and lost you felt after you first learned of your child's diagnosis? Your family is going through a similar emotional roller coaster.

I don't mean to make things out to be dire here. The fact is that your family can still be the core of your social support system. All they need is a little training and guidance. Your job then is to provide that training and guidance. Try some of the following:

> Share your research with your family. Spend time teaching them about your child's condition.
> If and when they voice erroneous assumptions about your situation, kindly, but firmly correct those assumptions. You can be forthright without being mean, and this forthrightness will help your family learn.
> Give family members specific assignments related to your needs. If you wait for them to come up with ideas of what to do for you… you will be waiting a LONG time for help (remember, they don't know how to help you yet). By telling them what to do, you give them a chance to help in a way that is useful to you and helps better educate them through experience. Over time, they will get a better idea of you and your child's needs.

Here are a couple of examples of how my wife and I put these principles to use with our kids:

First, you all should know that I have been blessed by the *World's Greatest Mom* (aren't they all?) -- heretofore to be referred to as WGM. WGM is a former special education teacher who has been nothing but supportive in our efforts to foster and raise our children. Now, despite her experience and support, she has never lived with autistic kids. Consequently, while she wants nothing but to support and help us (since she loves all our kids and she loves getting to be grandma to so many great children), she doesn't always know what to do.

In one particular case we noticed that family get-togethers were getting very difficult for us. Our two autistic boys just needed more support when we went to WGM's house with everybody there. There were more people, more food… in short, too much stimulation and too many changes to expect perfect behavior all the time. What was happening is that I was spending a lot of time hanging out in the car de-escalating a child while the rest of the family. Basically, one or both of our boys would get over-stimulated and start to tantrum and then we'd go to the only place available to us that was free from too many people, too much noise, etc. (our minivan).

Eventually, my wife and I told my Mom how difficult these family get-togethers were for us, WGM took that information and went out of her way to create a quiet room for our kids. She set aside a room in the house and stocked it full of quiet activities for the boys. The result? We had a place to go to get away from the noise and decompress. Now, no one had to leave the party. The boys had a place to decompress without feeling punished. Pretty soon, the whole family was taking turns hanging out with the boys when they wanted (wanted… not had to go) to the quiet room.

My other example involves WGM and my oldest son who is diagnosed with ADHD. Number one son was struggling at school with his homework. In true ADHD fashion, he was completing assignments and forgetting to turn them in, half doing assignments and generally not working up to his potential. Eventually, despite all my best efforts, I was at my wits end. Every email from a teacher just left me feeling helpless. I turned to WGM and asked for her help. I told her we needed to figure out a better way to motivate my son to use his organizational strategies. I didn't know how, but what we were doing clearly wasn't hitting the mark.

WGM took to this assignment with gusto. She put together an incredible program of rewards and check-ins that dovetailed nicely with the reward and check system we had in place at home and in school. The result? Number one son started getting his work done more consistently and his grades started climbing back up. It was a beautiful thing to witness. The extra reinforcement and motivation provided by WGM resulted in improved self-esteem for Number one son as well.

In both examples, I asked for help from WGM. I didn't tell her exactly what to do (I wasn't sure what would work). However, because WGM had some knowledge from her background as well as from my wife and I as to how our children "tick"… she was able to come at our situation from a different perspective and see solutions Lorrie and I missed. You can do the same.

Educate your family like you educated yourself, then ask them for help. It may be that you have to tell them exactly what you want them to do. It might also be enough to say you are stuck with a situation and see if they can give you some useful input or bring something new to the situation. How you go about it doesn't matter as much as that you don't let yourself get stuck in a situation alone. Create your social safety net. Nurture it and help it grow. This, more than anything will help you find success in your parenting efforts.

C. … Do the same thing with your friends.

All the steps you took with your family, you can take with your friends. Educate them. Tell them what you need. They will want to help, give them the tools to do so.

D. …Make a book that holds all your child's info

Get yourself a 3-ring binder, the biggest you can find. You may need several if your child is older and you have a lot of past paperwork. You are going to divide this binder into sections. **The first page should be a"face sheet."** It should include a recent picture of your child (within the year), identifying information (height, weight, eye color, hair color, identifying marks, etc.), Current medication list, allergies (if any), likes/dislikes, emergency contact information, insurance information. Try to keep it to one page if at all possible. This sheet (or a copy) should go with your child to every medical appointment or meeting with a provider.

Other sections should be (at a minimum) **home, school, medical**. In each section, put any pertinent paperwork, report, etc. that you have. Keep everything. Keep it in the book so it's easy to find. Don't throw out old reports when they get updated. Again… KEEP EVERYTHING. If the binder gets full, start a new one. This information will prove invaluable to providers as they come and go from your life. It will also help to document treatments that worked, didn't work, etc. Don't rely on your memory. It is unlikely you will remember the specific dosage and schedule of something like a medication your child took when he was 10 when you talk to a new psychiatrist 5 years later.

Update the face sheet at least annually. Make sure the demographics and picture are within a year. Pick a date such as a birthday, the first of the year or whatever to do this.

Another thing to put in this book , after the face sheet is a "care plan." This should be a quick narrative summary of the child that includes likes, dislikes, preferred activities, and guidelines on how to handle any challenging behaviors your child might display (include both slow and fast triggers, environmental factors, and potential reinforcers to use or avoid). If there are particular training or behavior protocols being used with your child, include those as well. The purpose of this plan is to have something to give to new people in your child's life such as babysitters, respite providers, etc.. so that they know how to interact with your child in an appropriate, nurturing and healthy manner. Update this plan at least annually as well.

Erik Young, M.Ed., LPC

5. CONNECT WITH AVAILABLE COMMUNITY RESOURCES

You need to expand your social support network beyond your family and friends. There is, most likely, a host of community based supports that will make your life as a caregiver easier. The problem is that how to access these supports (and that they actually exist) can be tricky to navigate. It is imperative that you do your homework and develop your advocacy skills so that you and your family can access the supports to which you are entitled.

A. Be in contact with community groups, support groups, county/state agencies, etc. Find out what services and support they offer.

Your first stop should be checking in with your local, county, state and federal offices. Every region has different names for the appropriate agencies. Here in Pennsylvania, you are looking at the Department of Public welfare, the county intermediate units (associated with the education system), and other similar agencies (mental health, Bureau of Autism services and so forth). These agencies are mandated to provide support to you and your child. Finding the appropriate agencies and their contact info can be daunting… but in this, Google is your friend. I like to do a search that includes the diagnosis (autism for example) the phrase "support services" and the zip code. From there, I will try to find promising links and then follow that link to other potential services. If at all possible, hook up with a social worker in one of these agencies, this person will likely know about other agencies and can provide appropriate contacts for you.

Additionally, look into parent support groups. There are various support groups for just about every condition under the sun. Attending meetings with these groups can be a valuable source of education. Many of these parents will not only be able to tell you about the various support agencies in your area, but will probably have personal contact information for key people at these agencies. It may be hard for you to get out of these meetings regularly due to your child's needs and your busy schedule, but at least make the effort to make the connection to other parents. You guys can support each other... and these people will know EXACTLY what you are going through. They will have insider knowledge of the people you can trust and the people you need to avoid. Networking with them can help you avoid time and money wasting mistakes.

You should also get connected with your local school system as soon as possible. Even if your child is not school age yet, you want to get to know the various administrators, school psychologists, special education teachers, and others. You want them to get to know your child. That way, when your child enters the school system, both they and you will be familiar with each other. Trust me, this will make transitioning to school services later so much easier. Additionally, some school districts offer early intervention services. These services will allow you to access assessment and testing. They may also be able to provide you with some targeted interventions in the form of specialized pre-school. This is incredibly important because the sooner your child starts receiving therapeutic interventions, the better the outcomes are likely to be. The literature is very clear on this. There is very little benefit to be had from putting off treatment.

B. Be the squeaky wheel... advocate for yourself.

Unfortunately, the community services you are looking for cost money. When things cost money, then there will be lots of regulations and people tasked with being gatekeepers. Their job is to make sure only those who need the services get the services so that money can be saved. This is not necessarily a bad thing, but it leads to you having to jump through some hoops to get access to what you need.

In some cases (social security for example) you will almost certainly be denied services the first time you apply. You will be forced to go through an appeals process and really press your case to get access to the services.

In other cases, you will have to fill out reams of paperwork and provide extensive documentation to prove your case. Each agency will have different regulations, and often they don't play well with each other. In the end, accessing the services and support to which you are entitled can be confusing and daunting .

So, BE THE SQUEAKY WHEEL. Make some noise. Rattle some cages. Ask for what you want and don't take "no" for an answer without a really good reason. In my experience, the parents that do this get things done.

On the news in recent weeks has been the case of a young girl with end-stage cystic fibrosis. There was no child donor lung available to her, though she might match with an adult donor. However, due to her age this was a problem. Her parents lobbied doctors, lawyers, senators. They started a massive social media campaign that went viral. Pretty soon the regular media was reporting on this child. In the end, a judge made a decision to allow this girl and another young boy to access the adult list and she got her donor lung. Why? Her parents made some noise.

Now, you don't necessarily need to create a national viral social media campaign to get services, but you may need to reach out to all sorts of people (like lawmakers). You may need to stay in frequent contact with various agency representatives just so that your child's name stays fresh in their minds. You will need to learn to network. By doing so you will make connections. (Remember your social safety net? Yeah, it's nurtured by networking.) These connections will allow you to access the community services to which your child is entitled. It can also open up surprising avenues for help and support.

C. Don't take "No," for an answer. Be persistent.

When you start to advocate and network, you will often hear "no." While there may be times that you will have to accept that as an answer, don't accept it every time… and not without a strong justification.

****

TRUE STORY!

My wife and I had the experience of going rounds with my son's school when he was 16. He was doing poorly and his ADHD symptoms were posing serious problems for him. At his IEP, they gave us a plan that was pretty much like the plan he had the year before. Our reaction was, "If that didn't help before, why do it again?" We were unhappy, but to do?

I decided I needed to treat this just like a case at work. When I get stuck with a client at work, I find it often helps to start fresh and take things back to the beginning. In this case I decided to do an FBA (Functional Behavior Analyses… you can read more about this process in section three of this book). The behavior I examined was Zak's habit of half doing, not turning in, or outright skipping homework. Despite all our efforts, the school's efforts… Zak just could not stay on top of his work. He could do most of it when he chose to do so, but that doesn't matter if the work doesn't get turned in and graded. We tried numerous reinforcement and organization systems, self-management plans...and they worked, so long as we (his parents and teachers) pretty much did the work for him. As soon as we tried to transfer the responsibility to him he would ultimately get off track, fail… and to make matters worse, hide it and lie about it. This led us down a pretty rough path with lots of negative consequences. In the end, it felt like he didn't care. We all started responding in kind.

Looking at my analyses, I had to figure WHY Zak was behaving the way he was. What was the reinforcement? It had to be pretty powerful for him to accept the negative consequences he was receiving. I looked very carefully at all the data I collected and it finally started to make sense. This was a case of *negative reinforcement*. Years of lots of little failures surrounding his struggled managing ADHD in an environment that is antithetical to the ADHD brain (high school) had created a negative self-image combined with a high degree of anxiety.

Zak felt pretty miserable much of the time in school. He didn't understand some assignments (those were often just flat out ignored), he started a lot of assignments then got off track (those were the ones where some things didn't get turned in). His coping strategy was to simply put these failures out of his mind and go do something that felt good (play video games, do an assignment he liked, watch tv, etc.) He was so good at it that once he put something out of his mind it he never thought of it again until someone else brought it up.

So, thinking about school work led to lots of anxiety, forgetting about school work led to no anxiety. Furthermore, when things eventually got to a point where he had to face it, lots of people (parents, teachers, etc.) got roped into helping him fix it. It was a few days of super high anxiety with help, compared to a long period (sometimes weeks) of no anxiety at all. The absence of anxiety was reinforcing his school work habits.

Based on this analysis, the best avenue seemed to be to prevent Zak from escaping from his anxiety-provoking stimuli. We had to make him do his work no matter what. The plan we presented to the school was as follows:

1. Every teacher would notify us when the work was not being turned in (even if it wasn't being graded… such as parts of larger projects).
2. They would stop lowering his grades for late papers.
3. We would make sure that any assignment we were notified about would get completed.

Seems pretty reasonable, no? The school was not a fan. They didn't think they could get all the teachers to up the communication level, nor could they see why they shouldn't ding his grades to teach him a lesson. I pointed out that dinging his grades had not motivated him so far and was simply increasing his anxiety and low self-esteem (thus working against what we needed to do). It took several meetings (all called by us) to finally get the school to see the logic of my analyses. We compromised on points 2 and 3… once notified of missing work, we had until Friday of that week to get the work turned in for a grade. After that, there would be penalties.

It took some doing. We had to stay on the school to hold them accountable for communication. We had to stay on Zak to get the work done (he was not a happy camper at first). However, his grades started going up. Then, something unexpected happened. The daily emails slowed to a couple a week… then to a couple a month…. then to nothing. No emails saying Zak forgot something or didn't turn in work. No more emails saying he lied when confronted about not doing his work. Not only that, but his grades stayed up (solid B's). By the middle of his Junior year, Zak was cruising on autopilot. His demeanor and affect was improved. We even found he had an aptitude for chemistry and writing. This continued with only minor bumps in the road through his senior year until graduation.

****

The moral of this long, long drawn out tale is that we didn't accept no for an answer. We didn't just go with what the school wanted and we were able to work out a compromise that changed our child's life for the better. You may have to do a lot more work up front, but this will often lead to much less work and stress later. Remember, you know your child best.

D. Don't be afraid to try to create resources for yourself.

Another thing to do is think outside the box and look for opportunities to create the resources you need (instead of trying to find others to supply them to you). This is not necessarily an easy thing to do. It takes persistence, resources and time. However, what better way to guarantee that your child gets what he/she needs than to create it for them?

It could be something as simple as creating your own Picture Communication Book using pictures you took with your camera to help your non-verbal child to communicate. It could be something like when I redid the walls in my boys' bedroom so that they would stop putting holes in them when they got angry (rather than pay $$ for a handyman). In one special case, I met a woman at an autism conference who couldn't find an appropriate group home for her adult son who was diagnosed with autism. Rather than just accept what was there, she went and found out what was involved in running a group home. With that knowledge, she went and started a formal group home just for her son. With this she was able to define what program the home would run, hire and fire staff… complete control over her son's needs. Now, I'm not saying you need to go to this level for your child, but know that it's possible.

E. Look for unexpected resources (outside the box thinking)

Finally, be on the lookout for help in unexpected places. You never know where the next connection in your social safety net will be. Helpful connections can come from anyone at anytime. You need to keep your eyes and ears open and do not be afraid to talk about what you need and who you are. People can't help you if you keep your needs to yourself. Case in point, I recently joined a business networking group to help grow my private practice. As I do a lot of family work and child work, I would be connecting with the family law attorney and maybe the chiropractor in our group. However, it turns out the electrician got me some of my first referrals. As it so happened, our electrician was a foster parent and on the board of a local foster parent group. When he heard about my specialty work, we immediately connected and he started sending me referrals. It was what I was looking for, but it came from an unexpected source. I never would have figured an electrician would have the kinds of connections I needed.

Erik Young, M.Ed., LPC

6. STRIVE FOR BALANCE – THE ART OF SELF-CARE

Be there for yourself, so you can be there for your child.

> *We, as parents, are willing to sacrifice ourselves for our children. But, let me ask you this... who takes care of your children when there's nothing left of you?*

When your child has exceptional needs, it can be overwhelming. You may often find your child's situation taking over your life. At times, this is necessary... but sometimes it isn't. Sometimes our desire to just be doing something (even if it isn't actually making a difference or helping) is what keeps us sane. However, that kind of grind typically comes at the expense of self-care. We, as parents, are willing to sacrifice ourselves for our children. But, let me ask you this... who takes care of your children when there's nothing left of you? If you can't be there who will? For this reason, it is *imperative* that you learn to care for yourself so that you can care for your child. Your self-care is as much one of your child's needs as his other needs... maybe even more so.

Think about it. Increased stress leads to compromised immune response (you get sick easier), poor sleep, impaired thinking, increased depression/anxiety, and a host of other negative consequences. If you have all that going on, you are not going to be as effective as you normally would be as a parent. This, in turn, will probably lead to increased stress... increased stress symptoms... worse parenting... where does it end? It ends when you decide to end the cycle and work some self-care into your daily routine. Again, think of self-care and part of your child's care.

A. Manage your stress –

Self-care is truly all about stress management. Everyone has stress. It's a normal part of life. Unfortunately, your circumstances probably come with greater (or at least different) stressors than most. So, managing and minimizing stress is the key to your self-care.

Stress management involves two things.: 1) Solving specific problems to reduce stress (which I can't really address in this book) and 2) making lifestyle changes that increase resiliency and inoculate you against increased stress. That is what this section summarizes.

1. Sleep

Sleep is perhaps the most important thing you need to reduce your current stress level and inoculate against future stress. If you are not getting enough sleep (or more to the point, enough *quality* sleep) then negative consequences are almost immediate. Lack of quality sleep makes it hard to think and concentrate. It leads to increased irritability and decreased ability to make decisions. Your energy is shot. Your ability to enjoy life is gone. I've heard that going one night without sleep impairs you as much as a few alcoholic drinks (in driving scenarios at least). Think about what this does to your ability to be there for your child and meet his/her needs?

So, if you are not getting enough quality sleep, then correcting that has to be on the top of your self-care list.

> ➢ Aim for 6-8 hours of quality sleep each night.
> ➢ Take naps when you can, but they DO NOT make up for lost sleep.
> ➢ Make your room conducive to sleep. Dark, quiet, and comfortable.
> ➢ Try to keep to a regular sleep schedule if at all possible.

➢ Avoid eating right before bed.
➢ Avoid exercising right before bed.
➢ Use deep breathing, meditation, or some other relaxing activity right before bed to decrease sympathetic nervous system stimulation.

2. Nutrition

What you put in your body can have a huge impact on not just what your body looks like… but how it functions. Eat a balanced, nutritious diet, and you will generally inoculate yourself to stress. Eating a lot of the foods we know are unhealthy leads to poor physical health which can aggrevate and activate all sorts of stressors. Poor diet makes us more prone to depression. So, eat your vegetables. Make sure you get enough protein. Eat a moderate amount of healthy fats. Limit starches and sugars.

Chances are that even if you eat pretty well you still aren't getting enough of everything you need. So, take a good multi-vitamin. Also supplement with Omega 3 oils (if your doctor approves)… these are shown to not only help reduce joint inflammation, but improve brain function.

3. Exercise

Exercise is so beneficial, it's right up there with sleep as a way to inoculate and manage stress as far as I am concerned. The health benefits of regular exercise are well documented and I won't go into all of them here. For our purposes, regular exercise increases energy, immune system health, and brain health. When we exercise, endorphins (the natural feel-good chemicals made by our body) are released. This counteracts the effects of too much stress on our system. Basically, regular exercise is a natural anti-depressant/anti-anxiety intervention. Regular exercise promotes better sleep (assuming you don't do intense exercise right before bed). The bottom line is if you aren't regularly exercising, then you are not as able to manage the major stressors in your life.

Keep in mind, I'm not a personal trainer or fitness expert… just an enthusiast. I have found in my own life that when I exercise I function better and feel better. I'm a better spouse, parent, and professional.

I am also crazy busy. I'm sure you are too. How to fit in something like exercise into that busy schedule without adding stress? Here are a few guidelines for working exercise into your lifestyle:

- Think about exercise as a necessity not a luxury. It's something that keeps you sane and allows you to parent at your very best.
- Do what you can and do things that you enjoy. If you don't enjoy running.... don't run. Conversely, if running is your thing... then go for it.
- Schedule it and stick to that schedule. You only need something like 30 minutes 3 times a week of moderate exercise to gain a lot of benefits. It's doable.
- Do a variety of things. Switch your routine up occasionally. If all you do is run outside, what are your options when the weather is bad? What are your options when the gym is closed? Personally, I have 5 or 6 different routines I cycle through and I'm always looking for new things to try. It keeps me motivated and staves off boredom.
- Try some sort of sport and work your routine around that. Being involved in a sport will get you out among other people (which will help keep from having your children consume every aspect of your life) and you can then tailor your workouts around the needs of your sport.
- It doesn't matter so much what you do so long as you are moving and doing something. Do what you enjoy and enjoy what you do.

4. Meditation/Prayer/Contemplation

There is evidence that regular practice of meditation or prayer activates the para-sympathetic nervous system (i.e. helps you relax) and reduces/staves off stress. This can be another great tool to improve your self-care. Spend a few minutes each day in prayer or meditation (whatever feels most comfortable to you). It doesn't have to be fancy or require a specific technique. Just spend some time with a quiet mind and just be in the moment. Practice this and you will improve your mental and physical health.

5. Forgiveness

No one is perfect. None of us always succeed in doing the right thing at the right time all of the time. Life is confusing and messy. There are few things of which I am certain and one of them is that we will all screw the pooch at one time or another.

While this seems very bleak… it isn't. It's liberating. We don't have to hold ourselves up as some sort of "super parent." We are just doing whatever we need to do to get from one day to the next. If we screw up, so be it. It happens. Fix it and move on. Part of "fixing it" includes forgiveness, especially to yourself. Carrying excess guilt just increases the stress. We have enough of that. No need to add to it when we don't have to do so. Be a good enough parent. Get it right most of the time. When you don't, fix it, love your kid, love yourself, get through the day and start fresh the next day.

6.   Comparisons -- possibly true but definitely unhelpful.
This seems to be a fundamental quirk of human nature. We compare ourselves to one another. I first noticed this at the gym when I was working out. I would notice who the big strong guys were. Then I would start feeling bad about myself because I was not big and strong like them. This irrationality ignored the fact that these guys had been working out for years and years and what I saw was the result of a lot of hard work I had yet to put into my own body. Eventually, I learned to focus on myself and compare myself to today with myself from yesterday… as long as I was improving on what I was working on, all was good. I learned what to do from watching the big guys, but didn't base my self-worth on that.

A similar thing can happen to parents. We look at what another child is doing compared to our own and maybe feel bad because our child is struggling. Or maybe a parent is doing something we would like to do..so we feel bad because we aren't doing it. This sort of comparison, while it may be based on some level in truth, is not particularly helpful.

> *Children with special needs are not a homogenous group. Even when they share similar diagnostic features, there is a lot of variability between children. So much so as to make comparisons pretty meaningless in my experience.*

Children with special needs are not a homogenous group. Even when they share similar diagnostic features, there is a lot of variability between children. So much so as to make comparisons pretty meaningless in my experience. Furthermore, that same level of variability exists between families. I remember right after my son was diagnosed with ADHD lots of people advocated changing his diet to eliminate artificial food colors, gluten, and other things. The fervor on this was almost religious in nature. If we weren't following this restrictive diet… we were bad parents (or that's what it seemed like at the time). We tried to do this. Truth be told it's a hard thing to do. These restrictive diets are very difficult to adhere to. When my wife and I compared ourselves to other families doing this… we were failing. We felt bad.

Here's the thing, even when we were 100% compliant… out son's symptoms didn't change. Once we dropped the family-to-family comparisons, we were able to see that this (for us) was a waste of time and money. We could then better focus on other things that would be helpful to Zak. I would say to you as a special needs parent, don't compare your child to other children. Don't compare yourself to other parents. Do what I did in the gym. Learn from other parents but don't compare. Compare your child to him or herself. When something you try shows improvement. Keep it. Otherwise let it go and do something else (even if everyone else in your circle thinks it's the next big thing.)

B. Be proactive –

Being proactive means planning ahead. In general, the more proactive you are the better. The opposite of proactive is being reactive. Reactivity means that bad stuff has already happened and you have to deal with whatever it is. Being proactive generally means less stress (you already have a game plan) and quicker response to bad situations compared to being reactive. Here are a few things you can try to do to increase proactivity and decrease reactivity:

1. Scheduling – Be disciplined. Create some structure out of chaos.

Truth be told, this is one of the best strategies I've found to keep my life manageable, but it was one of the hardest ones to master. I am, by nature, an improviser. I am most comfortable "going with the flow" so to speak. I like to fly by the seat of my pants. That being said, this is a bit of a reactive stance and can only take one so far. When I started really mastering the art of scheduling it felt weird and unnatural but it simplified many things for me in the long run. Now, many of you are probably not like me… you might already be natural schedulers. You might be very uncomfortable with going into a situation with a vague game plan and going with the flow. Regardless of your inclinations, being able to schedule is important. How much you do is up to you.

What does scheduling look like? For me, I carry a personal organizer. If I need to be somewhere or something needs to be done, I enter it into the scheduler. I keep it with me at all times and it beeps at me to remind me to be somewhere or to get tasks done. Most modern smart phones and computers have applications that will help you do this. Alternatively, a pen and paper organizer can work just as well (I need things to beep at me to prompt me… I sometimes get so busy I forget to look at paper organizers). I make it a habit to look at my schedule first thing in the morning to kind of map out my day and prioritize what needs doing. From there I can set goals based on what absolutely has to get done (high priority), what needs to be done soon (medium priority) and what would be nice to get done but is not critical yet (low priority). A good day for me means the high priority stuff was addressed or delegated and maybe I did some stuff on the medium priority list. If I get to the low priority list… then it's an outstanding day!

In addition to the daily "triage" as I call it, I sync my calendars and check for accuracy on a weekly basis. You may or may not have to do this. In my case I am juggling my private practice calendar/tasks, my work calendar/tasks and my home calendar/tasks. Sometimes these three calendars don't mesh well. Synching them up regularly helps minimize conflicts and stays on top of last minute changes.

Of course, I'm not the only one with a busy schedule. My wife has her stuff, as do each of my kids. To that end, my wife keeps her own schedule (she's more a pen and paper gal…. doesn't really use her smart phone apps). Then we keep a centralized calendar at home. Each of us has been assigned a color and then our stuff is put on the family calendar by color code. That way, at a glance, we can see who needs to be where and do what. As my wife is the keeper of most of this we just use one of those big desk calendars that you can get at any office supply store. I know other families who use something like Google and keep a family calendar to which each member of the family can add stuff. No matter how you choose to do it, **make sure everyone commits to doing it.** This will help decrease conflict and increase the ease of planning.

Another thing scheduling can do is if your child is autistic (or otherwise very ridged in how they approach and deal with the world) it can decrease anxiety. Using a visual schedule (pictures as well as words) will allow you to help decrease their anxiety about what is coming up and help them plan for future events. There is an article that goes into this and other ways to make transitions easier in the third part of this book.

2. Plan for the worst, expect the best.

I'm betting you're thinking "that seems a little dire." Maybe, but I'm not suggesting you go catastrophic (make mountains out of molehills). Simply ask yourself, "Realistically, what's the worst that can happen?" Then try to have some sort of contingency plan for that. Once that's done, expect that everything is going to go smoothly going into the situation. In my experience, the worst rarely comes to pass (but when I was prepared for it I was always grateful!) and I often get something very close to the best (just because that's what I expected… what researchers call "experimenter bias").

I've used this strategy so much it's become second nature. I often do it without thinking. For instance, when I go out with my kids, I always have an "exit strategy"--- a way to leave the area should one of my children not be able to handle the situation or otherwise become upset. I know my children's warning signs for tantrums and aggression and I know (depending on the child) what I can handle on the spot and what behaviors are signs that it is time to leave. I always note the nearest exits. I'm mentally prepared to do things like leave a full cart of groceries near the checkout line because it's time to go. I'm prepared to leave a movie theater in the middle of the movie because it's time to go. **I do so without resentment and minimal frustration because that's what we do.** That being said, I generally can take my kids anywhere and we have few problems because my kids are awesome and expect them to be awesome. I don't know how much they "get" that… but I'm only rarely disappointed. What I'm saying is that the preparations for disaster free you to not have to worry about them. They let you drop the anxiety (been there, can deal with that) and this lets you then focus on the positives. I think kids then pick up on that positivity and respond in kind more often than not.

1. Flexibility – be ready to adapt to surprises (despite all your planning)

I like to collect funny T-shirts. One of my favorites is a black shirt with white, gothic lettering. It simply says "manure occureth." Shit happens. Two little words that succinctly sum up a fundamental fact of life. No matter how much proactive planning we do… life is going to find a way to throw us a curveball. You have an important doctor appointment but your car won't start. You plan a special day with your child, but he comes down with the flu. How to deal with things such as this? Be flexible and improvise. Do the best with what you've got and DON'T PANIC.

Now as I noted earlier, I am not a natural scheduler (though I've learned to do it), but I AM a natural improviser. When the unexpected happens, I am in my element. Conversely, if you are natural planner, facing unexpected changes can be very daunting and anxiety provoking. The first thing to do is assess the situation. What's the most pressing issue? Can it wait? What resources do you have at your disposal? What resources can you realistically get your hands on? Based on all of this, come up with a plan and make a decision. Then repeat as necessary until the surprise is resolved… then get back to your original plan if possible.

Flexibility and pre-planning go hand in hand. Pre-planning reduces the number and the intensity of problems with which you have to handle. It gives you more energy and resources to throw at unexpected problems. Flexibility allows you to adjust your plan or even abandon it all together when the circumstances warrant. Frankly, it's a lot of mental gymnastics. Just stay calm, take a few breaths and make the best choices you know to make given your circumstances. Once that's done, then don't beat yourself up if things fall short. Learn from the situation and work that back into your proactive planning for future use.

**God grant me the serenity
to accept the things I cannot change;
courage to change the things I can;
and wisdom to know the difference.**

-- Reinhold Neibur

That is the serenity prayer. This is my mantra. By adopting this mindset you can hit that magical balance between structure and flexibility. This mindset allows you to let go the things you can't do anything about right now. You get to absolve yourself of all that guilt. It empowers you to take charge of that which you can manage. If you can hit this balance, you will be a good enough parent, good enough partner, good enough you... and that is all anyone can aspire to. You can do it. I believe in you.

7. SERIOUSLY…DON'T PANIC!

'Nuff Said.

Erik Young, M.Ed., LPC

PART TWO: BONUS ARTICLES

Erik Young, M.Ed., LPC

WHAT'S UP WITH MY CHILD'S BEHAVIOR?: A PARENT'S PRIMER ON FUNCTIONAL BEHAVIOR ANALYSES – PART 1

Parenting is tough. It is perhaps the toughest job in the world. We give everything of ourselves for the well-being of our children. If our child has special needs such as Autism, ADHD or some other neuro-behavioral condition, the degree of difficulty rises exponentially. With these children, the answers aren't necessarily in the standard parenting books.

I don't know about you guys, but I can't tell you how many times friends and colleagues have either politely changed the subject or given me the dreaded "what the hell do you do this for?" look when I tell them about what my kids have done (hint: I have a line item in my yearly budget for replacing toilets...I have to do that once or twice a year on average...). The bottom line is if your kid has special needs, the usual avenues of family and friend support is often not helpful in getting advice to resolve behavior issues. While they mean well, our family and friends often lack the knowledge and experience to give us sound support and advice for our unique circumstances. In this article I want to help you to help yourselves. You aren't alone and you have the tools to deal with many of the situations your child will throw your way.

What to do when your child is doing something you don't understand? Why is he drinking entire bottles of ketchup in the middle of the night (true story)? Why is he writing his name in poop on the wall (also a true story)? Why on earth is he doing homework but not turning it in for a grade (seriously...another true story)?

Step one: Take a deep breathe.

Step two: DON'T PANIC!

Step three: Ask yourself this question, "Why?" In counseling circles we ask "what is the function of the behavior"? (Yeah, we like to use 15 words where one will do...go figure) The answer to this question is going to give you a lot of insight as to what is going on and help guide you in your efforts to deal with the situation.

Entire books have been written on how to do this and future report will deal with different aspects of this process. However, for right now, take a close look at the **W's.**

WHEN does the behavior occur?

WHAT happens before, during and after the behavior?

WHO does the behavior happen around?

WHERE does the behavior tend to occur?

Based on that analyses, see if it fits with the following common functions of behavior:

To get something: People do things to get things. It might be a toy, it might me attention, it might be food, etc.

To get something to stop: People do things to get stuff to stop. For example, I just told one of my kids to quiet down because they were distracting me while I wrote this article.

To escape something: Similar to the previous function. If we don't like the activity we are doing, we will do things to get away from it.

It feels good: We tend to do things that feel good. Go figure.

It's a reflex: We don't have much choice with these behaviors (startle reflex for example).

There are other behavior functions, but these categories cover most situations. It's important to figure out the function because missing this step can make your attempts to deal with the situation less effective at best and possibly make things worse. For example, a child that runs away from you every time you want him to do chores is going to need one kind of intervention if you figure the function is escape (making him finish the task but giving a big reward for completing it) as opposed to if the function is attention (withdrawing attention except when the child is "on-task").

I hope this information helps make your day to day challenges less challenging. Please feel free to email me at erikyounglpc@verizon.net with any comments, questions or suggestions. Next time we will talk about reinforcement. Hang in there parents and remember, BREATH and DON'T PANIC! You got this...

Visit me at www.erikyoungcounseling.com to find out more about myself and to schedule an appointment.

Reinforcement: The Power of Rewards

A Parent's Primer on Functional Behavior Analyses – Part 2

In the first report, we talked about how figuring out why someone is doing something is key to changing their behaviors. We learned that most behaviors happen to get something, get away from or stop something, because they feel good or because they are automatic (a reflex for example). In this article we will learn about reinforcement which combined with the answer from the question "what is the function of the behavior?" will allow us to change the behaviors.

Case Example:

So, imagine this scene...one that is played out in countless grocery store everyday around the world. Picture, if you will, one harried mother trying to get the grocery shopping for the house completed. She is tired and in a rush to get home. With her is her young son. In the checkout line, as Mom tries to load the groceries on the little conveyor belt, her child asks for a candy bar (located conveniently at child eye level right there on the shelves in the checkout). Mom, being a kind and benevolent Mom, says "No, we're going home and having dinner. You don't need a candy bar right now." Her son, being like most children of his age, doesn't really like this state of affairs. In response to the benevolent denial of sucrose refreshment, he starts wailing at the top of his lungs, "PLEEAAAASEE!! I WANNA CANDY I WANNA CANDY I WANNA CANDY!!!" Other store patrons stare at the impending debacle...this is a familiar scene. Mom feels embarrassed and more than a little ticked off. She still has to get the groceries home, get them unpacked and start making dinner. Dealing with a tantrum is the last thing she wants to do. At first she tries to calmly explain to her child about dinner, the child screams louder. Then she commands him to cease his tantrum. That works about as well as can be expected (i.e. not at all). Finally, Mom gives in a buys her little angel the candy bar, at which point he immediately ceases his caterwauling.

Pop Quiz: Can you name all the reinforcement that occurred in the above example? What do you think will happen the next time Mom brings her son to the grocery store?

WHAT **IS** REINFORCEMENT?

The technical definition of reinforcement is *anything that occurs after a behavior that increases the chances of that behavior occurring again in the future*. Simply put, when your child does something (a behavior) and you do something immediately afterwards, if your child repeats the behavior again in the future…whatever you did was a reinforcer.

This idea is key to behavior change. We want to provide rich and powerful reinforcement for the behaviors we wish to see (Start behaviors) and we want to avoid reinforcement for the behaviors we do not wish to see (Stop behaviors). This interaction is at the heart of everything we wish to accomplish.

IMPORTANT POINTS

- Reinforcement only occurs if you see the behavior again. You might feel you are rewarding your child, but if the reward does not result in increased frequency, intensity or other improvement in the behavior…then the reward is NOT reinforcing.

- Reinforcement can be anything. It doesn't have to be a pleasant thing either. For example, a person who likes fighting might enjoy when he is in a fight and find getting hit or yelled at reinforcing.

- Reinforcement ALWAYS increases behaviors. Anything that decreases the chances of seeing a behavior is called a punisher.

The bottom line parents is, reward your kids when they do what you want them to do and they will do those things more. If you simultaneously remove the rewards from the behaviors you want to see less of, you will see less of those behaviors.

ISN'T THIS JUST BRIBERY?

Short answer – Nope.

While bribery is used to change behaviors there are some key differences between bribery and reinforcement. Bribery is typically something (often money) given to someone in advance of behavior. It is always given to get that person to do something unethical or illegal. Reinforcement always occurs AFTER a behavior, and we are not using it to get our children to do anything unethical or illegal (hopefully!).

WHY SHOULD I BE REWARDING MY KID FOR DOING WHAT HE IS SUPPOSED TO DO? SHOULDN'T HE JUST DO IT?

In a perfect world, yes, your child would do what he/she is supposed to do and I would be out of a job. However, I the real world, children are compelled by the "Drive Your Parents NUTS Accord" to not always follow directions. If we, as parents, want to keep our sanity, it behooves us to use all the tools at our disposal to encourage, reward and ultimately to TEACH our children what to do and when to do it.

TYPES OF REINFORCEMENT

- **POSITIVE** – The most common type. It is something that is added to the situation (money, candy, praise). Basically, if you give your child something because he did something good...that's positive reinforcement. In the case example, the mother positively reinforced her child's checkout line tantrum behavior by buying him the candy.

- **NEGATIVE** – This NOT punishment (that decreases behaviors). It is the removal of something. In the case example, the child negatively reinforced Moms candy bar buying behavior by ceasing his tantrum when she gave in and bought the candy bar.

CLASSES OF REINFORCERS

- **PRIMARY** – These are typically those things that all people need. Food, air, companionship, etc. Often tied to basic survival. These are good because most everybody will respond to them. However, they suffer from the "too much of a good thing" effect – also known as satiety. When you've had enough of something it loses its reinforcing qualities.

- **SECONDARY** – These are learned reinforcers. Typically paired in some way with primary reinforcement, these can be anything. Money is perhaps one of the most prevalent secondary reinforcers in the world. It always amazes me what people will do for colored bits of paper.

OK, SMART GUY, WHAT DO I DO WITH ALL THIS INFORMATION?

Follow these simple steps:

1. Ask yourself; is this a start behavior or a stop behavior? (Do you want to see this more or less often?)

2. Ask yourself, what is the function of the behavior?

3. For stop behaviors, the answer to that question will tell you what you need to decrease or eliminate from the situation to make the behavior go away. Do that.

4. For start behaviors, the answer to the question will tell you what you need do to get the person to do that behavior more (or better).

As with all things simple, there is a lot more to look at, but it all comes down to these four points ultimately. We will discuss more about reinforcement and how to set it up and deliver it in future articles.

WHAT'S THE BEST REINFORCER?

The best reinforcer is the one that works in a given situation. However, I do have a preference for a particular kind of reinforcement: PRAISE. I will cover praise in more detail in a future article. However, here is why I like praise as a reinforcer, just about everybody responds to praise. The more you praise someone, the more they like you. The more they like you, they more they will respond to you. Praise is free. It takes up no space. People rarely get tired of it. It pairs well with every other kind of reinforcer (thus making the praise and the other reinforcer more effective).

So, in your experiments with reinforcement, try adding a little praise to your efforts and see how it enhances things.

I hope this information helps make your day to day challenges less challenging. Please feel free to email me at erikyounglpc@verizon.net with any comments, questions or suggestions. Let me know about creative ways you have found to reinforce you children (or anyone else for that matter). Hang in there parents and remember, BREATH and DON'T PANIC! You got this...

Visit me at www.erikyoungcounseling.com to find out more about myself and to schedule an appointment.

CONNECT WITH YOU CHILD USING THIS SIMPLE TECHNIQUE: PRAISE!

In today's article, I want to talk more about my favorite reinforcer: PRAISE.

PRAISE IS SPECIAL!

- ➤ It's FREE!
- ➤ It's abundant.
- ➤ It's easy to store.
- ➤ Everybody likes it.
- ➤ Like chocolate or bacon….it goes with everything!

The bottom line is that you cannot praise your kids enough. In fact, the more you praise them, the more you will see those "start" behaviors!

GUIDELINES TO PRAISING EFFECTIVELY

Here are some tips to make your praise better:

- ➤ Make sure you have the child's attention…use their name. If the child doesn't know you are talking to him, then your praise is nothing more than wasted breath. This is particularly important when dealing with children on the spectrum who may not even know you are there even though you are standing right next to them. Do whatever you need to do to become a part of their world before you deliver your praise statement.

➢ Tell the child what they did. They might not be aware of what it was that they did that was so great. Maybe a lot of things are happening at once. In any case, saying what you are praising helps tie your praise with the behavior you want to see again.

➢ Be enthusiastic! If you deliver your praise statement in a low monotone voice, If you come off as being sarcastic, if you give any hint to the child that you aren't being sincere…the child will know it. Seriously, CHEER for your child. Get excited about what they did. Hell, be a little silly. Sell the sizzle and your child will respond more.

➢ Praise IMMEDIATELY! Deliver that praise as soon as the behavior occurs. The longer you wait to praise (or deliver any reinforcement for that matter), the less likely it is for the child to connect your praise to the behavior you want to see again. Even worse, the longer you wait, the more likely your child is going to do a "stop" behavior. It would be a shame to deliver a praise statement that gets tied to and reinforces a stop behavior…so don't do that.

➢ Flip the script occasionally. It's easy to get into a rut and basically deliver your praise in the same way with the same basic wording all the time. So, change things up often. Here's a link to "100 ways to praise a child" http://www.speechtherapygames.com/Freebies/waystopraise achild.pdf

➢ "Thank you" is no praise. I know this seems backwards…giving thanks is common courtesy. However, if thank you is in your praise statement, also add another praise statement with it. The idea is that by saying thank you, you are hinting that the child did you a favor rather than the child did something he/she should do all the time. It's a little thing, but no point in undermining yourself if you don't have to.

Here is an example of an effective praise statement:

Delivered immediately after child puts away a toy he

was playing with. (Enthusiastically) Good Job

Zak! You put away the toy. I'm so very

proud of you!

So, now that we know how to praise effectively, get out there and pass it on! Remember parents…Don't Panic, Breathe, You got this.

Please comment and tell me about ways praise has worked for you. Questions are also welcomed. I can be reached at erikyounglpc@verizon.net

Find out more about me and schedule a complimentary session at www.erikyoungcounseling.com

FINAL THOUGHTS

With the information in the first three parts of this report, you have all the tools to get your child to do more of what you want him to do and less of what you don't want him to do.

Step 1: Identify a start behavior and a stop behavior.

Step 2: Come up with a plan that reinforces the start behavior and

removes reinforcement from the stop behavior.

Step 3: Work the plan.

Step 4: Adjust the plan as necessary to keep things moving in the right direction.

I hope you found this information helpful. If you want help creating your reinforcement plan or would like more   direct support, then please don't hesitate. Go to www.erikyoungcounseling.com or email me at erikyounglpc@verizon.net to schedule a free consultation today!

Antecedent Modifications

(in "Normalspeak", changing what happens **before** the behavior)

Did you ever hear the old joke about the guy that goes to the doctor? He says to the doctor, "Doc, it hurts my arm every time I do this," (as he raises his arm). The doctor, looking thoughtful, says, "Well, don't do that!" I'll bet you're wondering, "What does an old vaudeville routine have to do with behavior modification?" Simple! By avoiding or changing the THINGS THAT TRIGGER behaviors, we can better manage them.

ABC's

Behaviorists describe behaviors in three parts labeled "the **ABC's**":

1. Antecedent,
2. Behavior,
3. Consequence.

 In the three-part free report, you learned about the Behavior (What is the function?) and you learned about consequence (reinforcement). This article will focus on **antecedents**...the things that happen before the behavior.

For practical purposes we are concerned about **two** things that happen **before** a behavior:

1. **Triggers** &
2. **Setting events**.

Triggers are the things that consistently cause the behavior to happen. For example, if someone jumps out and startles you, you jump. Analyzing the triggers allows us to answer the question: "What is the function of the behavior?". It also allows us to **predict when** a behavior is going to happen.

Setting Events (also known as "slow triggers") are situations and environments where the behavior is more likely to occur. Example: I am not much of a morning person. To get through the morning, I rely on set routines because my brain is not typically fully engaged when I first wake up. Change my routine even a little bit and I am more likely to forget things, become grumpy, etc.

What do we do with this information?

At the very least, if you understand the triggers and setting events of behaviors…you can use that knowledge to **eliminate** the behaviors by: 1) removing triggers and/or 2) avoiding setting events. Conversely, you can elicit desired behaviors by: 1) creating setting events and/or 2) putting triggers into the environment.

Try this to reduce "stop" behaviors:

➤ Write down all the possible setting events and triggers of the behavior. (You should have a good idea about this from when you were figuring out the function of the behavior).

➤ Now, for EACH event and trigger, ask yourself, "Can I make this go away?"

- o If the answer is yes, then take steps to eliminate stressor.
- o If the answer is "no", then ask yourself "Can I reduce this or make it happen less often?"
  - ▪ If that answer is yes, take steps to make the stressor less prevalent in your life.
  - ▪ If that answer is "no", then ask yourself, "What do I have to do to live with this?"
    - ❖ The answer to **that** question will lead to a CONCRETE PLAN you can follow. Simple…but not easy. Most good thing in life are like this.

Try this out and let me know how it's working for you. Above all, DON'T PANIC. Breathe. You've got this.

I welcome your questgions. I can be reached at erikyounglpc@verizon.net

Find out more about me and schedule a complimentary session at
www.erikyoungcounseling.com

Erik Young, M.Ed., LPC

The Power of Play

Play therapy at work

Play therapy has become a very important element of my work with families and children. In this article, I hope to give you parents some idea of how powerful play can be as an intervention as well as some ideas of how to utilize play with your own children.

It is Father's Day as I write this article and I am reminded of one particular case where play therapy had a profound impact on a family. This family had a child with severe autism. They were unable to manage him at home and he was living at the residential treatment facility where I worked. The child in question was very routine oriented and had an extremely restricted range of activities in which he would engage. Basically, if he wasn't repeatedly watching small snippets of Disney videos, he wasn't happy. To make matters worse, if he wasn't happy, he tended to tantrum, hit and bite those around him. As a result of these behaviors, not only could he not live at home but the family was challenged to even have him home for short visits. They literally had to put the entire house on lock down to prevent their son from wandering away and at least one of them had to take time off of work to stay up all night to supervise their son.

When this child came onto my caseload, I and another therapist decided we wanted to work with the family to improve the quality of their interactions with their son and make their time together less stressful and challenging. We decided to use a therapy called Theraplay to accomplish this. We did several sessions with the child in which we exposed him to various new activities. We made note of what he liked, what he disliked and what he just didn't seem to get (but didn't hate). We expected to see a lot of behaviors due to the change in routine, but that wasn't the case. We quickly found that there were a number of activities that the child seemed to enjoy. Furthermore, we found that a number of activities that he didn't understand at first he learned and started to enjoy in subsequent sessions. Pretty soon, we had a list of about 20 or so activities that required minimal material (about $20 of stuff from the dollar store) that he enjoyed. We could easily keep the child happily engaged for over 30 minutes at a time.

We then started doing sessions with the family at their house. First, they watched as we played with their son. Then we started showing them how to do the games. During the course of this session, we were demonstrating a modified version of catch. The child tended to want to catch the ball when thrown to him, but would then walk over and hand the ball back to you instead of throwing it. We learned that playing catch over a table got the child to actually throw the ball back. As we were demonstrating this, he started throwing the ball to his dad and playing catch with him. Dad immediately started tearing up. He said, "This is the first time I've ever had a catch with my child." Let me tell you, there was not a dry eye in the room after that. What Dad doesn't want to have a catch with his son? Imagine having to wait 17 years to have that happen? It was an unexpected, but awesome outcome of our therapy.

The importance of play in development

Play is one of the fundamental ways in which children learn. Through play, they learn to how to connect or form secure attachments to others. The quality of the relationships a child has as they grow up will impact the quality of the relationships they form as adults. So it stands to reason that good, quality play as a child can lead to good quality relationships in adulthood.

Through play, children learn how to self-regulate. We get excited as we play games with each other, but then we learn how to self-calm and soothe to continue to excel at the games we play. We learn when it is appropriate to get excited and when we need to calm. In fact, I find that using play with children who have problems with regulation is a fantastic way to teach them impulse control and self-control.

Finally, through play, we learn how to socialize. We learn such things as taking turns, cooperation, and competition. We learn about rules and creativity. Through play we develop the basic skills that allow us to navigate the challenges that life presents us. Kids who don't play are often at a great social disadvantage compared to kids who play.

Guidelines for play

Ok, so play is important. However, to maximize the impact of play on your child's behaviors, here are some basic guidelines to follow.

1. Play with your child

When engaging in play, do things that involve interaction between you and your child. It's not enough to be in the room as they play (what I call proctoring). It's great to sit with your child as they do a puzzle, but it's better to do the puzzle with them. You want to promote that social-emotional connection with you. You want to make yourself a source of never ending reinforcement in your child's eyes. So, do activities that promote things like touch and eye contact (something the typical autistic child might be struggling with and need practice to do or tolerate). Make the time your child spends with you silly and fun; watch how your child positively responds to you in other situations.

2. Keep it simple and developmentally appropriate

Make sure the activities you do with your child are geared towards their mental and emotional age. In the example at the beginning of the article, even though the child was 17, he enjoyed things like holding hands, rocking and singing "row your boat." He enjoyed the sensory nature of the rocking as well as the familiarity of the song. For a more neurotypical teenager, I might do something like sing and dance with them to music they like. Again, focus on enhancing the connection between yourself and the child.

3. It's ok to be silly (in fact it's recommended)

The games I play with my kids (at home and at work) aren't complicated. In fact, on the face of it they are pretty silly. However, I find that even with the most resistant, morose child... silly draws them in. There's something about being silly with someone else that just brings down defenses. Besides, taking time to relax, laugh and be a little silly is FUN... it's a marvelous way to spend some time.

4. Inexpensive is better!

If you've ever spent time shopping at the toy store, it's very easy to spend a lot of money on toys. Heck, expensive toys can be great... I adore my xbox… but for the types of interaction I'm thinking about, expensive toys are unnecessary. Blowing a feather back and forth, blowing bubbles, playing clapping games or "red light, green light" require very little in the way of materials. Be creative and see what kinds of things are sitting around your house and look to those for inspiration. Have you ever seen a young child at Christmas? They open up all their expensive presents and spend most of the time playing with wrapping paper and boxes. Tap into that instinct with your child and you will be well on your way to successful play.

Ways to use play therapeutically

Here are some more ideas on how to structure play sessions with your child to get specific results.

Planned sessions to increase engagement

While my usual play style is typically to improvise with whatever is at hand and make things up as I go along, I find that planning out sessions can be helpful when trying to engage with a child. I simply make a list of 5 to 10 activities that I want to do before I do the session and try to at least get through that. I make note of what activities seemed to get the child to respond positively to me so I can use them again later. If I don't do this, I tend to more easily get shut down by the child if he/she doesn't immediately engage with me. I focus on activities that promote touch, eye contact, and positive sensory experiences. Good examples are singing/clapping games, Blowing up a balloon while the child holds the balloon, and blowing a feather back and forth between your hands and the child's hands.

Repeated sessions to increase skills

If I am trying to help a child acquire or improve a skill, then I want to focus on repeating activities between sessions instead of changing things up frequently. Repeated exposure is good for skill acquisition. For example, I often use play to teach deep breathing through things like blowing bubbles, singing, and a game called "monkey ride" (where I put a stuffed monkey on the child's belly and then have him take a deep breath in and give the monkey a ride up to my hand which I place a couple of inches about the monkey's head). I will repeat these games and variations of them through several sessions until the child has mastered belly breathing.

Short sessions for planned breaks from difficult tasks (The head cooler)

When a child gets upset, frustrated or anxious during specific situations, play can be a great way to manage this. For instance, a lot of my kids have problems around homework. They get upset if there's too much, or they don't understand it, or even can't make themselves take a break because it's not done yet. The child then gets so upset they couldn't do the work even if they wanted to. The poor parents are not only stuck trying to calm an upset child, but then they face the daunting task of getting their child to return to finish the dreaded homework. Hours of this every night can be a major stressor for the whole family.

So, to counteract this, I suggest trying "lots of little bits." The parent works with the child to do homework, but also watches the child for the initial signs of agitation, frustration or upset. As soon as the parent or children notice them, they take a short break. During the break, they spend just a few minutes doing something fun and silly (no video games or other major distractions). The goal of the activities is to allow the child's head to "cool off." Once calm, the child returns to the homework with a clear head. Families that have been successful in doing this find that not only are there fewer fights and tantrums around homework, but that more homework is getting done in less time.

I hope you've found this information helpful. The bottom line is that play is important. The more challenges you face with your child the more important it is to put time aside every day to have some positive interactions….be silly and have fun. Please share in the comments section below your ideas for play or any questions you might have. In the meantime, play more with your kids and remember…. BREATHE, you got this.

Irritating thoughts: Change your thinking to reduce you stress

I.   What are "irritating" thoughts?

It happened to me during an end of semester performance at music school. I'd been working all semester on three pieces that my teacher thought would showcase my talents and stretch me a little bit. I had two pieces down solid, but the third piece, a Chopin etude was not fully memorized. My teachers said I should go ahead and just play it with the sheet music out as it highlighted my technical skills at the piano.

On performance day I made one crucial mistake. I did not have someone act as my page turner for that etude. As usual, nerves were high. I knew I was being graded and judged, so I was more anxious than usual. The first two pieces went well but it all changed during that etude. It started out ok. But then about half-way through my performance, I heard a thump in the ceiling and then felt a warm gust of air wash over me and the piano. It was the heat system kicking in. The air caught the corner of the page I was reading and started turning it. Next thing I knew, I was staring at the next piece in the book five pages from where I was playing. Did I mention I DID NOT have the piece memorized? I lost my place and my fingers started stumbling over the keys like drunken Irish clog dancers.

It was terrible. Immediately, my legs started trembling. I lost sensation in my hands. My heart was beating so hard I thought it might burst out of my chest like that creature for the movie "Alien." I was in full-on panic induced adrenalin dump. As I tried and failed to finish the etude gracefully this is the stream of consciousness that was running through my mind:

"#*&^$!! Oh no! I lost my place. My performance is ruined!! I've just been exposed as the worst pianist in the school. Everyone will know what a fraud I am. I'm going to fail this course. I'm going to fail the semester.

I'm getting kicked out of school. I won't be able to get a job. I'll lose my apartment. My family will leave me. I will die alone and broke."

Pretty crazy huh? In fact, everyone loved he performance and felt terrible that I had the bad luck to have my sheet music get disturbed by the heating vent. I got an A for the performance and kept my 4.0 gpa (I was never in any danger of failing anything). The thoughts that stampeded through my mind were examples of what I've come to call "irritating thoughts"

Cognitive behavior therapists call them "irrational" thoughts. I prefer to call them "irritating" thoughts, a concept I picked up from a fellow therapist. I find the former term implies something wrong with you while the latter term is more focused on what the thought does. We all have them. We pick them up throughout our lives like a long-haired dog picks up sticker-burrs running through a field. Sometimes they are thoughts that were necessary to mentally survive a particular situation that no longer fit the current circumstances For example, your thoughts on the opposite sex from when you are seven are not applicable to dating in your 30's. Other times they are messages we've absorbed from other people in our lives. Often, these thoughts are sub-conscious and automatic. They pop in and out of our head without our being aware of them. But these thoughts impact our behaviors and emotions in subtle yet powerful ways.

II. Mountains and molehills

In my piano performance, I experienced a cascade of irritating thoughts that took a small situation and a little panic was kicked up a notch by another thought that in turn led to more panic which led to more thoughts...with the whole thing spinning out of control in my head. It's the classic "making a mountain out of a molehill" situation. It's like your brain gets hijacked.

The problem is that when these cascades of irritating thoughts run amok, it activates the fight-flight-freeze reaction. The physiological response to this is fine if one is in a true life or death situation, but the limitations on language, planning, forethought combined with the effects of things like the stress hormone cortisol on our system are problematic when we are NOT in a life or death situation. In my case, while my disrupted performance was embarrassing, it was not life threatening. Reacting as if it were did not improve the situation and caused me undue distress. The fact of the matter is that many people have similar reactions all the time. In a sense, we pile unneeded distress and stress upon ourselves in addition to the actual stress that life throws our way as a matter of course. There is good news though. Just as our thoughts can trigger a stress response in our body, our thoughts can also trigger an anti-stress relaxation response. We can take control of that which feels out of control.

III.   Thought stopping

Thought stopping is a technique used in Cognitive-Behavioral psychology to change these irritating thoughts and thereby change your mood and behaviors. It starts by identifying when these thoughts are present. As a rule of thumb, when you feel nervous, anxious or irritable (especially when these feeling are not in proportion with what is going on around you) you can bet irritating thoughts are present. Learn to identify the early warning signs of an activated nervous system (for me , I usually feel it in my stomach first). Once identified, check in with your thoughts and listen to your self-talk. What are you saying to yourself? Are the thoughts logical? Do they fit what's going on? Are they leading to increased emotionality or are they calming?

In my example, the thoughts of how bad I played and how that would destroy my career and life were clearly illogical. They were out of proportion with the situation. Not only that, they were totally unhelpful. I needed to calm my mind and focus on my performance, but the thoughts running through my mind made that task darn near impossible.

So, be critical of your thoughts. They might not be true. They might not fit the situation. They may be true, but also unhelpful. In any of these cases you need to stop cascade in its tracks. The procedure to do this is pretty straight forward. Once the irritating thought is identified, you need to mentally yell "STOP!" if you are someplace where you won't be embarrassed feel free to say that out loud. To add an extra degree of impact, some people add a physical sensation to the stop to help interrupt the thought. I like wearing a rubber band on my wrist. I snap it a little bit as I think "STOP." This serves to distract my brain briefly and stop the thought.

IV.   Calming thoughts

The next thing to do is to replace the irritating thought with a calming thought. If you don't, the irritating thought will just start up again. By putting a competing thought in its place (one that is helpful and relaxing) you make it harder for that irritating thought to hijack your brain. For example, if the irritating thought is "I'm stupid. I can't do this," you should think about ways in which that thought is inaccurate (perhaps you've done this thing before with no problem so clearly are capable). In my example, the thoughts that I was a terrible piano player ere inaccurate because I had just played two pieces well…something a poor pianist could not do. If I'd tried to keep that fact forefront in my mind I might have been able to stay calmer and recover easier.

Admittedly, this technique takes some practice. If you are not used to thinking like this it will seem strange at first. For this reason, I invite you to take some time and practice it. Don't wait until you are feeling anxious and out of control…take time to check in with your thoughts when you are feeling relatively calm. You'll be surprised at what kind of automatic thoughts pop into your head. In doing this you will be able to start becoming aware of your irritating thoughts. Once identified, it is easier to notice when they are present. When you are calm, it's also easier to figure out what kinds of calming thoughts will best take the place of your irritating thoughts. By practicing when you are calm, it will be easier to put this technique into practice when you are not calm.

One final note on thought stopping, you should combine this technique with the stress management skills I have talked about such as deep breathing and deep muscle relaxation. By combining calming techniques you will be better to reduce your current stress and inoculate yourself against future stress. All it takes is a little practice and patience to take control and improve your quality of life.

I hope you've found this information helpful. I invite you to comment on how irritating thoughts have impacted your life and ways in which you've managed them. I also welcome any questions you might have in the comments section. Until next time, remember, Breathe…You got this.

Stress

(and some ideas on what to do about it)

Stress - everybody seems to have it (or knows someone who does) - and nobody seems to want it. This makes sense, as excess stress can adversely impact one's health (physical and mental). Left untreated and unchecked, it can become a life-threatening condition. In this article, we will discuss:

➢ what stress is and isn't,
➢ what purpose stress plays in our lives, and review
➢ some simple strategies to assess and manage our stress.

What is Stress?

I always tell my clients that *stress = change*.

Basically, whenever we are subjected to any sort of change in our environment, this is stress. In actuality, this is a bit of an oversimplification; **stress is really just our physical and mental reactions** to changes in our environment (rather than the change itself). So it is more accurate to say that stress is positively correlated with change. It's out innate way to deal with danger (real or perceived). This is an evolutionary survival mechanism.

➢ When the stress changes **fall within** our capacity to adapt, then we become faster, stronger, smarter, etc.
➢ When the stress changes **exceed** our capacity to cope, that's when bad things happen.

Symptoms of over-stress include:

• Low-energy
• Restlessness
• Shaking/nervousness

- Aches and pains
- Frequent colds
- Feeling "run-down"
- Difficulty concentrating
- Racing thoughts
- Worry/anxiety
- Impaired decision making
- Impulsivity
- Irritability
- Rapid weight gain/weight loss
- Procrastination/avoidance
- Self-medicating (increased use of drug/alcohol)

Good Stress vs. Bad Stress

Believe it or not, **stress is not inherently a bad thing**. In fact, lack of stress can be as bad as too much stress. Think about it, stress is a reaction to change. Without change there is stagnation...no growth. Without growth, we wither physically, emotionally and mentally. A little bit of stress, applied strategically is the secret to becoming a stronger person (physically, emotionally and mentally).

Take for example the weightlifter. He/she goes to the gym and lifts weights. This is a stressor to the body. The muscles get worked (in fact the activity causes little tears in the muscle tissue). If done right, the weightlifting then triggers an adaptive response so that s the weightlifter rests, the muscles repair themselves and do so in a way that makes them grow bigger and stronger.

Another example would be taking a class. The stressor is going to the class and doing the assigned work. This stimulus forces one to think differently and take in information. Done right, we learn new information and incorporate that into who we are. This can in turn impact how we think, feel and behave....growth.

I've got too much stress. What do I do?

First things first. We need to take stock of what is going on. By figuring out where you are, it is easier to figure out where to go from there.

I. Get yourself five pieces of paper.

    a. At the top of one piece of paper put the heading **Environmental**." Underneath that, list all the stressors that are in your environment. For example, is the house too cold? Are you in the middle of nasty weather? Is your space cluttered or disorganized? List everything about where you are at (or where you spend a lot of time) that is a source of stress to you.

    b. Do the same with the other sheets of paper using the headings:

        i.   **Physical** (are you sick, hurting, injured, etc.),

        ii. **Inter-personal** (are you in a fight with a spouse or a friend? Are you lonely? Are you overwhelmed by obligations to others? Feeling lonely or isolated?),

        iii. **Work/School** (too much work to do? Don't understand your assignments? Behind on your work? Not enough work to do? Under paid?), and

        iv. **Cognitive/Behaviors** (What are your thoughts about yourself? Are you engaging in behaviors such as excessive drinking and risk taking? Are you being too impulsive? Are you feeling anxious or scared? Depressed?

II. Next, circle or highlight the top one or two stressors. It is best to focus on just a few things to change at a time rather than trying to do everything at once. Putting a lot of effort into a small, targeted area will create more change faster than spreading your efforts around too much. I find that once I get movement on a couple of key stressors, a lot of other situations resolve themselves (often because they are tied to the big stressors I already took care of).

III. Now that you've identified the key stressors that need work, you must make some choices. For each stressor, ask yourself the following questions:

1. **Can you avoid or eliminate it?** If so, what are the consequences of this solution? It makes no sense to embark on a solution that creates more problems than it solves. A good example of eliminating a stressor is if you feel hungry, eat something.

2. If it can't be eliminated, **can it be lessened or reduced in some fashion?** As an example, my daughter is prone to stomach pains. Consequently, we avoid certain foods that trigger her issues and reduce how often and how intensely they occur.

3. **Can you reframe it or think about it differently?** I feel this strategy often gets overlooked. How stressful a situation is has direct correlation to the amount of worry and importance we give it. By changing how we think about a situation, we can increase or decrease how stressful that situation is to us. As an example, a guy cuts me off in traffic. If I take it personally and think, "What a jerk!" I tend to get angry and stressed out. However, if I remind myself to not take it personally (I don't even know the guy) and think of alternative explanations (maybe the guy is having a bad day himself, maybe he's dealing with an emergency, maybe he simply didn't see me because I was in his blind spot or something), then I tend to have a more sympathetic mindset and experience less stress.

4. **Can I learn to deal with the situation?** Sometimes we have to seek help from other sources to deal with things. That's ok. If I learn techniques to understand and manage a situation I go from being overwhelmed to being in control. This may take time, but is often a stellar option to choose.

5. **Can I live with it?** Sometimes life isn't fair. Things happen and there simply isn't anything to be done. In these cases it's best to accept that you cannot change things right now. Work on your patience. Keep checking in with yourself and hopefully things will change and you will be able to employ one of the other options to resolve the stressor. Engaging in

excessive worry and spinning your wheels in this situation then becomes a waste of time and energy that can be better used resolving other stressors.

At the end of the day, I find the Serenity prayer really sums up what we need to do to manage stress:

God, grant me the serenity to accept the things I cannot change,
The courage to change the things I can,
And the wisdom to know the difference.

    -- *Reinhold Neibur*

Next time I will go into some specific tricks to reduce and manage stress. In the meantime get working on your stressor inventories. I hope this information proves useful. Breathe....You got this.

Please leave your tricks for managing stress in the comments section below. For more information or to make an appointment, go to www.erikyoungcounseling.com or email me at erikyounglpc@verizon.net

Copyright 2012 by Erik Young, M.Ed., LPC

Erik Young, M.Ed., LPC

Baby Steps – Using micro-change to make major changes

What about Bob?

I love movies. Watching movies is one of my favorite off-task activities. Since I'm a therapist, it probably comes as no surprise that I have a fondness for movies that involve therapists. Of those movies, one of my favorites has to be the Bill Murray/Richard Dreyfuss comedy "What about Bob?" True, the portrayal of Dreyfuss as a therapist is less than flattering… but the movie is hilarious. At the beginning of the movie, Dreyfuss gives Murray's super-neurotic character, Bob some advice. He tells him to take "Baby steps." Do one little thing, then do another little thing…. Keep going until you get to where you want to go. Using this advice, Murray is able to leave his apartment and make his way "on vacation" to New England where he then intrudes upon Dreyfuss' family vacation. Much hilarity ensues.

Now, it might seem strange to take therapy advice from a goofy comedy, but I've always said that good advice is good advice regardless of the source. Frankly, the idea of making big changes by taking lots of little steps makes sense to me. Back when I was a piano teacher, there would always come a time where my students would start freaking out over learning their first long piece. "It's TOO long! I can't do it!" Is what I would hear. I would ask them a question my mom posed to me when I was young. I would ask them, "How do you eat an elephant?" Inevitably, they would scrunch their faces up, think about it… then say "I don't know." The answer is "ONE BITE AT A TIME." Like baby steps in "What about Bob?" you eat an elephant (i.e. Tackle a big problem) by taking the first step (or bite) and then do the next thing and the next until you get to where you need to go (or there's no more elephant left). What if you aren't hungry for elephant? Then I guess you're out of luck.

Defining micro-change

This idea of taking lots of little steps to solve problems is what I've come to term "micro-change." Big changes take lots of work. Big changes take lots of planning. Big changes take significant sacrifices and resources to make them happen. This is why people often avoid making big changes or start but never succeed in completing big changes in their lives. How many times have you thought how nice it would be to have something about your life be different, but when you sat down and looked at the situation you said, "Nah, too much work." I know I've done this more times than I like to admit.

Using micro-change we take a different approach. We decide on a goal (something big or long range) and then simply decide on what the first steps are going to be. Then we focus our efforts on the first easily attainable objective. We focus all our efforts like a laser on accomplishing that objective. Once it's done, we then move on to the next step. We don't spend a lot of time thinking about the end goal or how long it's going to take. We just focus on where we are and what we are doing until we get the step done.

I like to use this strategy with diet and exercise changes. Instead of saying "I need to lose 50 pounds, deadlift 500 pounds and get to 12% body fat." (All measurable and attainable goals... but pretty big and daunting all at once). I might say, for the next week I'm going to go to the gym at least twice and stop drinking regular sodas." What seems less daunting? It's really hard to lose a lot of weight. It's really hard to lift heavy. It's easy to cut back on sodas (and thus calories) for a week and commit to going the gym a couple of times. At the end of the week I can look back and see exactly how I did and then set new short term objectives. If every week I lift a little more than the week before while cleaning up my diet a little more, I will lose weight and get stronger. Making all the lifestyle changes needed to lose a lot of weight is scary and confusing, but making one small change at a time and giving the change time to become a habit is easier.

I've used this same strategy to teach kids how to organize for school and get on top of homework. I've used this strategy to help people overcome anxiety and fears (also known as gradual exposure therapy). I've become a big fan of doing "lots of little bits" to get "big bits" done. My motto is "keep it easy."

Guidelines to implement micro-change strategy

So, here are some tips on how to plan out and use this strategy to make changes in your life or your child's life.

Pick clear, well-defined goals (measurable)

For this strategy to work, you need a clear target.... Something to shoot for. While having a goal of "being happy" is nice, what does that mean? What's happy for you? How would I, as your therapist, be able to quantify and measure happiness? Is it how often you smile? Is it how many friends you have? **Pick a measurable goal.** "I will lose 20 pounds" or "I will see 16 clients a week" are measurable. Whatever it is you want to change, focus on those things you can count, and craft your goals around that.

Additionally, make sure you make note of your baseline when you start. It's important to know where you are at so that you can see where you are going as you make your goals.

Break goals up into smaller objectives

This is the essence of micro-change. Figure out the steps you need to take to accomplish your goals. Sometimes, you will be able to map the whole process out from beginning to end. At other times, you may be able to figure out the first steps, but later steps may not be clear (depending on how those first steps go). Either way, figure out small, attainable first steps and take action to accomplish them. For that 20-pound weight loss goal, cutting out sodas might be a great first step, followed by cutting back on starchy carbs and then upping protein intake. Making one change a week will lead to a virtual overhaul of one's eating habits in the space of a month or two. In the case of "seeing 16 clients a week" a goal might be to publish 2 articles this month (and then do it again next month) to get my name out there. Another step might be to schedule a free community talk based on one of my articles in the next month to attract new clients.

Pick realistic target dates

Give yourself deadlines. If you have an objective but no end date, it becomes very easy to procrastinate and put things off. By giving yourself deadlines, you add a little bit of urgency. However, **it is crucial that your target dates are realistic.** Losing 20 lbs in a month is not a realistic target date. Losing 6-8 pounds in a month becomes more realistic. Cutting out soda for a week is easy.... Cutting out soda forever might be impossible. I can always re-commit to no soda week after week as long as that change is helping meet my goal. If anything, it is better to be a little more liberal with your target dates just to give yourself enough wiggle room for success.

Collect data on progress

Since your goals are measurable, it makes sense to measure them. If you don't, how do you know if you are making progress? I can make the goal of losing weight... but if I never weigh myself, measure my body, try on old clothes that did not use to fit... how do I know I'm making progress? What if I'm making progress and then I choose a change that doesn't work? If I'm collecting data, that will be reflected and I can make adjustments to my plan sooner.

Reward yourself and celebrate your little victories

Finally, you need to make every effort to reward yourself and celebrate your successes. It might not seem like a big deal that you cut out soda for a week. It's such a little thing. However, you made a commitment and you met it. That deserves a pat on the back. We are creatures that thrive on reinforcement. That's what drives our behaviors. So, reinforce your positive changes. Celebrate your daily victories and be proud of yourself. This will help keep your enthusiasm and motivation up while you transform your life.

So, take those baby steps. Eat that elephant. Celebrate the little victories and change your life! I know you can do it. Please tell me about times you've changed your life with micro-change in the comments section below. I look forward to hearing from you.

If you wish to learn more about micro-change or would like to schedule a free consultation with me, please call 484-693-0582 , email me at erikyounglpc@verizon.net or click on the "schedule appointment" button on the right side of this page.

©Erik Young Counseling LLC

Erik Young, M.Ed., LPC

ABOUT THE AUTHOR

Erik is currently a clinician for the Devereux Foundation who specializes in working with children and teens diagnosed with autism, intellectual disability and behavior disorders. Twelve years ago, Erik and his wife decided to try to take what they know worked in the clinical setting and apply it at home. To this end, they started to provide foster care for special needs children. The result has been a sometimes frustrating, but always enlightening and wonderful roller coaster ride.

Erik quickly learned that what was possible in the clinical setting was not always workable in the home setting. He learned that even when the behaviors were manageable, life with an autistic child is very different from that of the neurotypical child. A fact that is not always apparent to his fellow clinicians. Today, he combines this hard-won personal experience with what he knows works in the clinic to help families support their loved ones. He loves being the parent of his special "crew" and he wants nothing more than to help other parents love what they do too.

When not doing therapy or parenting, Erik enjoys martial arts, exercise, making music and woodworking. Go to www.erikyoungcounseling.com to read more free articles from Erik or to schedule a free consultation.